Garfield's
ALL-ABOUT-THE-
FOOD
JOKES

Scott Nickel and Mark Acey

Garfield created by JIM DAVIS

LERNER PUBLICATIONS ◆ MINNEAPOLIS

What are the two things Garfield can never eat for breakfast?
Lunch and dinner.

Lerner Publications Company
An imprint of Lerner Publishing Group, Inc.
241 First Avenue North
Minneapolis, MN 55401 USA

For reading levels and more information, look up this title at www.lernerbooks.com.

Design elements: sabelskaya/iStock/Getty Images; Guzaliia Filimonova/iStock/ Getty Images.

Designer: Susan Rouleau-Fienhage
Lerner team: Laura Rinne and Lauren Cooper

Library of Congress Cataloging-in-Publication Data

The Cataloging-in-Publication Data for *Garfield's All-about-the-Food Jokes* is on file at the Library of Congress.
ISBN 978-1-5415-8980-3 (lib. bdg.)
ISBN 978-1-72841-344-0 (pbk.)
ISBN 978-1-72840-023-5 (eb pdf)

Manufactured in the United States of America
1-47490-48034-10/29/2019

What's Garfield's favorite kind of book?
A cookbook.

Why did Odie bring Jon a pair of bananas?
Because Jon asked Odie to fetch his slippers.

Why is Jon's cooking like a volleyball?
You can serve it, but you can't eat it!

If Garfield were a vegetable, what kind would he be?
A couch potato.

What's Garfield's favorite fairy tale?
Beauty and the Feast.

WAIT . . . YOU MEAN THAT FEAST WASN'T ALL FOR ME?

Did you hear the one about the red pepper?
It's hot stuff.

What do anteaters like on their pizzas?
Ant-chovies.

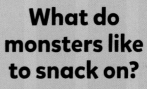

What do monsters like to snack on?
Ghoul Scout cookies.

What kind of cake do mice like?
Cheesecake.

Why wouldn't the other foods listen to the sandwich?
The sandwich was full of bologna!

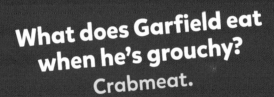

What does Garfield eat when he's grouchy?
Crabmeat.

What happened when the banana met the ice cream?
The banana split!

On what day does Garfield cook hamburgers?
Fry-day.

If Garfield had ten doughnuts in one paw and nine doughnuts in the other, what would he have?
Big paws.

Where does Superman shop for food?
At the supermarket, of course.

What do frogs drink?
Croak-a-cola.

What does a shark eat with peanut butter?
Jellyfish.

What is Garfield's least favorite cake?
A cake of soap.

I'VE RARELY MET A CAKE I DIDN'T LIKE

What would you get if you crossed a dinosaur with a pig?
Jurassic pork.

What would you get if you crossed a dog with a pizza topping?
Pupperoni!

What happens to Garfield when he eats a lemon?
He becomes a sourpuss.

MONDAYS ALSO MAKE ME A SOURPUSS

What would you call an overcooked sirloin?
A mis-steak!

Did you hear about the new ice cream for monsters?
It's called Cookies and Scream.

What did one egg say to the other?
"Heard any good yolks lately?"

What would Nermal be if he ate Garfield's dinner?
He'd be history!

Did you hear about the clam who didn't have any friends?
It's because he was so shellfish.

What happened when Garfield met the pan of lasagna?
It was love at first bite!

What kind of food improves your vision?
See-food!

What is Garfield's favorite kind of tree?
Poultry!

What's round, chocolatey, and swings through the trees?
A chocolate chimp cookie.

DID SOMEONE SAY COOKIE?

What is Santa's favorite Easter candy?
Jolly beans.

Why did the baker quit making doughnuts?
He was sick of the hole business.

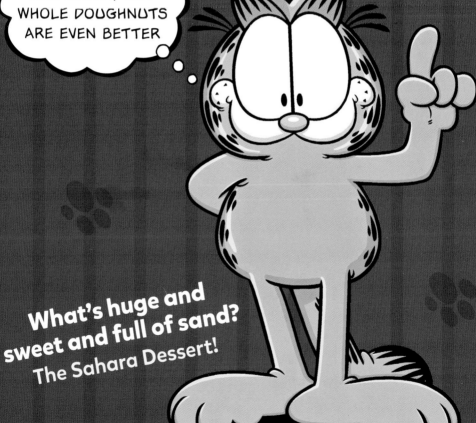

DOUGHNUT HOLES ARE GREAT, BUT WHOLE DOUGHNUTS ARE EVEN BETTER

What's huge and sweet and full of sand?
The Sahara Dessert!

What did the gravy say to the mashed potatoes?
"I've got you covered."

What is Garfield's least favorite pasta dish?
Spaghetti and mothballs!

Where does Queen Elizabeth shop for her dinner?
Get real! She makes her servants do it for her.

What is Jon's favorite food?
Anything Garfield doesn't steal from him!

How does Garfield eat a big meal?
One shovelful at a time!

What is Odie's favorite dessert?
Pooch cobbler!

What do you call a lizard who's a vegetarian?
A saladmander!

What crime did Garfield commit at Thanksgiving dinner?
Pie-jacking!

What is Garfield's favorite type of dog?
A hot dog!

Why are dogs like hamburger?
They're both sold by the pound.

Did you hear about the dog who could cook breakfast?
His specialty was pooched eggs.

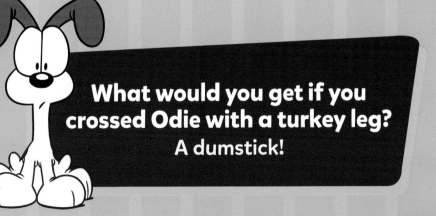

What would you get if you crossed Odie with a turkey leg?
A dumstick!

Why did the farmer jiggle the cow?
He was trying to make a milkshake!

MILKSHAKES AND CHEESE—TWO REASONS TO THANK A COW

Who is Garfield's favorite movie star?

The Blob. Garfield likes anything that can eat a whole town!

What's a duck's favorite breakfast cereal?

Quacker oats!

What kind of dog would make a good deli snack?

A beagle with cream cheese!

What is Garfield's favorite thing to put in a pie?
His teeth!

What is Odie's favorite movie snack?
A big box of pupcorn!

What is Garfield's favorite time to eat?
Anytime!

How many meals does Garfield eat each day?
As many as he can get!

What do penguins like in their salad?
Iceberg lettuce.

What did the toast say to the knife?
"Stop trying to butter me up!"

What animal goes "Gobble, gobble, gobble"?
Garfield at the dinner table!

IT TAKES TALENT TO EAT AS MUCH AS I DO

What did the man get when he accidentally sat on the hot stove?
Rump roast!